MARTI BLEDSOE POST

The Playbook
for Modern Moms

Retrofit

Retrofit: The Playbook for Modern Moms

Copyright ©2019 by Marti Bledsoe Post

All rights reserved.

No part of this book may be reproduced, stored in a retrieval system, or transmitted by any means, electronic, mechanical, photocopying, recording, or otherwise, without written permission from the copyright holder.

For ordering information or special discounts for bulk purchases, please visit a-parently.com.

Book design by Jenn Bajec
Photo credits: p. 6-7 Israel Palacio on Unsplash; p. 8-9 Alexander Lesnitsky from Pixabay; p. 20-21 Seb [P34K] Hamel on Unsplash; p. 32-33 Jeff Sheldon on Unsplash; p. 36-37 NeONBRAND on Unsplash; p. 38 Rudy and Peter Skitterians from Pixabay; p. 46 DepositPhotos; p. 50 William Stewart from Pixabay; p. 62 PublicCo from Pixabay; p. 64 PoloX Hernandez on Unsplash; p. 68 Keith Johnston from Pixabay

If you purchased this book without a cover you should be aware that this book is stolen property. It was reported as "unsold & destroyed" to the publisher, and neither the author nor the publisher has received any payment for this "stripped book."

ISBN 978-0-578-55686-4

Printed in U.S.A.

First Edition

Marti Bledsoe Post

To Marisen and Carson,
who showed me my heart.

Table of Contents

1. The Power of a Story — 02
2. How Did We Get Here? — 16
3. Work is Harder Than Ever — 30
4. Homefront, or Front Lines? — 44
5. Parenting is Hard AF — 58
6. The Way Forward — 74

CHAPTER 1

The Power of a Story

Recently I was asked to stand up and give a *tell-all* talk about working motherhood at an industry conference in my hometown.

My first answer was a resounding *no*.

I felt unqualified. I am, in fact, a mother of two kids and I was, in fact, working at the VP level at a digital marketing agency. But so-called *Imposter Syndrome* can even make you forget facts sometimes.

I felt afraid. I would be surrounded by peers in my industry, many of whom I would know personally. Instead of comforting me, this terrified me.

I felt vulnerable. I figured if I told the truth about how hard it was for me to be a marketing executive and a mother, I would never work in my town or my industry again.

And then, I did it *anyway*.

I did it because I realized other moms must feel as scared as I did, and someone had to broach the topic. Inspired by *A Short History of Silence*, by Rebecca Solnit, I realized if more of us didn't speak up, working motherhood would continue to be idealized and impossible while working mothers themselves completely overwhelmed and overlooked.

As the session grew closer, I talked to a number of other working moms, to see if my own story was maybe particularly hard, or particularly stressful. I thought it was my kids, or my husband, or even my boss or company that made my situation so unmanageable.

What I heard, in focus groups and interviews and lunch conversations, was that we all felt like somehow we weren't able to get *working motherhood* quite right. Even women in the same company, who all knew each other and knew about each other's kids and families, confessed that while they vented to each other regularly, they didn't really open up about their underlying fears and concerns.

So, emboldened by the idea that I was standing up for working moms everywhere, I stood in front of a crowded room and told the truth about my life as a working mom:

That it was hard. That I was scared. That I didn't know what I was doing most of the time. That my life moved so fast sometimes, I felt like I was on a treadmill and nobody would get hurt as long as I didn't fall off.

I told the truth about the toll on my marriage, the financial strain we faced even in a dual-earner household, and the way all the stress impacted my health. I think I said the *F* word about one hundred times. It felt very raw and real, and wickedly scary.

I opened myself up for questions at the end, and there were so many hands in the air I didn't know where to start. Women asked me tough questions, such as, *Where did you find the time to read a book about this topic?*

Eventually, moms within the audience began to answer each other while I just stood at the front, quiet and a little shaky. Even the few men in the room chimed in.

The conference organizers had to kick us out of the room, and I realized that although many of us had great circles of

I do not have this figured out.

influence in our careers and great friends in our personal lives, everyone needed just one woman to stand at the front of the room and say, *I do not have this figured out.*

We needed more than just a vent session, more than a funny, made-for-the-water-cooler-anecdote about a forgotten lunch or a miscommunication with the nanny. We needed to hear the real story. More importantly, we needed to hear it in a professional setting.

The sad feelings of missing out on our kids' pivotal moments, the threatened feelings of watching others' career moves, the incredible feeling of inadequacy and guilt that permeated everything.

We also needed some creative ways to process our stress and start to take action—because obviously drinking more wine and making more jokes about it wasn't solving the issues.

As the session ended, I realized it felt really good—really freeing—to have told the truth.

My wish is that it will feel just as good for you, and that this book will help.

Who is heard—
and who is not—
defines the status quo.

Rebecca Solnit, *A Short History of Silence*

FEELINGS IN FOCUS

You don't have to stand up at a conference and give a talk on being a working mom, but take a minute and picture your primary emotion about life at home. Draw a picture (or emoji!) that represents your feeling.

FEELINGS IN FOCUS

And now draw a picture of your primary feeling about work.

> Something powerful happens when you ask a woman to *share her story*

Melinda Gates, co-founder of the *Bill and Melinda Gates Foundation* and author of *The Moment of Lift*

FRAMING YOUR STORY

Now that I've shared some of my own working motherhood story, here is space and permission—and a template—for you to explore your own. This format is adapted from Pixar's renowned storytelling framework. I invite you to share this with anyone who needs to really *see* you in the heart of this amazing and agonizing life stage.

Once upon a time, I was _____

_____

_____

My life was _____

_____

_____

FRAMING YOUR STORY

On the day I became a mother, _____

_____

_____

_____

My life was _____

_____

_____

_____

Because of that, _____

_____

_____

And because of *that,* _____

_____

_____

Now, _____

_____

_____

FOR FURTHER READING/LISTENING

The Double Shift Podcast*
Hosted by Katherine Goldstein

This is feminist journalism at work, telling the stories of working moms beyond their careers or their kids.

** The author is a funding member of **The Double Shift.***

Just Let me Lie Down: Necessary Terms for the Half-Insane Working Mom
By Kristin van Ogtrop

This dictionary-style book is filled with funny and heartfelt definitions and stories from the former editor-in-chief of *Real Simple* magazine.

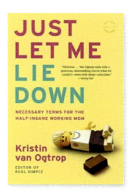

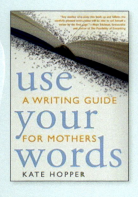

Use Your Words: A Writing Guide for Mothers
By Kate Hopper

Babies have baby books. Now you have a mother's book.

If you've ever thought of creating motherhood memoir pieces, or even just need a way to describe what has happened to you, this book will help you get started.

Notes: _____
_____
_____
_____
_____

CHAPTER 2

How Did We Get Here?

We've been on a collision course for generations.

In other words, this day was coming, and the women who are currently navigating child-rearing and career are the ones who will bear the brunt and the ones who must call for change.

We will look back and recognize this as the cultural flashpoint in which the expectations of families in general—and mothers in particular—are in direct opposition to our expectations of workers.

Over the past several generations, the expectations of mothers have risen beyond all logic or reality, to a level our grandmothers (and even our mothers) couldn't recognize. Across the majority of human history, raising children was, in fact, the work of a village. In her book *Inventing Motherhood,* Ann Dally points out that only since the mid 1900s have we considered it natural for a woman to stay home alone with her children.

You mean it hasn't always been like this?!

This cultural narrative developed as a result of World War II, attachment theory research on child development, and even economic trends such as the rise of homeownership following the G.I. Bill.

It greatly benefitted the patriarchy for this narrative to take hold. It also drastically lowered mothers' expectations of finding support to help raise their offspring so they could continue to pursue their own careers.

MOTHERHOOD

PRE-VICTORIAN: Survival

Back when our foremothers were having their babies, they couldn't plan or space their pregnancies and large families were needed for a steady supply of help for the agrarian economy. In those days, motherhood was a simple fact and childhood was simply a short period of mini-adulthood, full of hard labor and dangerous responsibilities. Young children were surrounded by siblings, grandparents, aunts, uncles and cousins, and the mother was simply one of many caregivers.

VICTORIAN: Madonna & Child

In the Victorian era, the ideal of the Madonna and child took over the cultural narrative and motherhood became associated with the highest expression of femininity. The qualities of nurturance and being a *true mother* were idealized, despite the fact that the mother herself was still a part-time caregiver, surrounded by hired help if she was wealthy, or by an extended network of other helpers if she was a working class mother.

A BRIEF HISTORY

POST-WWII: Primary Mothering

The rise of the middle class and the end of WWII really changed the game. Fewer women had help in their homes and many were isolated in new suburban tract homes. Attachment theory research conducted during the war inaccurately depicted the mother as the best and only source for children's emotional nurturing, education and psychological and physical development. In fact, the U.S. and Britain created an informational campaign to depict the mother at home. This narrative infiltrated popular content as well: just picture June Cleaver in her apron and high heels.

TODAY: Intensive Parenting

The New York Times has described modern parenting as *relentless*, and as women begin their careers before their families, they are less and less prepared to meet the demands of motherhood. Our philosophy now is that each child is precious, and the data shows that we spend more time, money and resources than ever before to get them to adulthood. Many modern couples aspire to be equal partners at home, and pay lip service to rejecting the ideal of the 1950s mother. And yet, data shows mothers still shoulder the majority of the childcare and home-related duties.

There have always been mothers, but motherhood (like childhood) was only recently invented.

Polly Young-Eisendrath, Ph.D.,
Women and Desire: Beyond Wanting to be Wanted

It's hard work to be a mother.
And a majority of us are also juggling jobs.

It's important to realize that by setting up the expectation that mothers should stay home alone with their young children, acting as the primary parent in the years before school begins, everything else began to look like a deviation from that ideal. This thinking sets up an emotional conflict for mothers, rather than brainstorming a modern support network for parents.

This wouldn't be quite so noteworthy on its own but for the fact that this has coincided with a rapid change in women's roles at work.

So, mothers who work full-time, mothers who go back to school, mothers who travel, mothers who work part-time, mothers who run for office or take a seat on the Board, mothers who train for marathons or go to the Olympics or serve in combat are all seen as doing those things *instead* of raising their kids.

The past 50 years have changed the face of the working population in the United States. Compared to about half in 1975, there is now a clear majority of women with children under the age of 18 who are in the workforce.

So, most of us are *working mothers*.

78%

of mothers with children under the age of 18 are in the workforce, vs. 48% in 1975.

Bureau of Labor Statistics, 2017

> The most labor-intensive style of mothering the world has ever seen... at the same time women entered the workplace and *began to achieve*

Juliet Schor, *How Women Rise*

40%

of women are the primary breadwinners for their households, compared to just 11% in 1960.

U.S. Department of Labor, 2016

TIMES HAVE CHANGED

Perhaps you've experienced this—a well-meaning mother or mother-in-law offers advice about child-rearing, suggesting that *babies haven't changed that much since it was my turn!* But the truth is, a lot has changed.

Name a few things your mom did when you were a kid that you cannot even imagine doing as a parent:

_____   _____

_____   _____

_____   _____

Has your mom or mother-in-law told you she can't fathom doing things the way you do? What are her primary examples?

_____

_____

FAMILY OF ORIGIN

Do you know the legacy of working motherhood in your own family? Have you and your mother or mother-in-law ever talked about the differences between generations?

Here are a few conversation starters:

- *Tell me about your jobs when your kids were young.*

- *What was the hardest thing about raising your children?*

- *Did you work or stay home before your kids went to school?*

- *Did you enjoy it? Or wish for the opposite? Or maybe both?*

- *What about your neighbors—were you surrounded by mothers who had a similar situation?*

- *Did you have child care options? Do you remember what they cost?*

- *How many hours did you work, and how much money did you make?*

FOR FURTHER READING

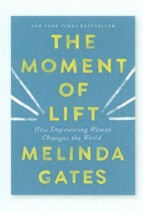

**The Moment of Lift:
How Empowering Women Changes the World**
By Melinda Gates

A bestseller in 2019, this will raise your awareness of global health trends and the way the simplest act of letting women control their bodies and pregnancies can literally solve the world's deepest crises.

**Making Motherhood Work:
How Women Manage Careers and Caregiving**
By Caitlyn Collins

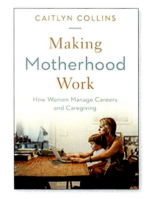

Another book hot off the presses—a 2019 publication detailing four years of research with working moms in Sweden, Germany, Italy and the United States. The similarities will surprise you and the differences will break your heart.

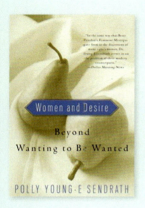

Women and Desire: Beyond Wanting to Be Wanted
By Polly Young-Eisendrath, Ph.D.

I was reading this book for a totally different reason—namely, to work on my own sense of agency beyond what society and men expect of me. But in these pages I stumbled upon the history of motherhood, got introduced to the work of Ann Dally, and my research journey really got underway.

The Cultural Contradictions of Motherhood
By Sharon Hays

This book, now almost 20 years old, was one of the first ones to examine how mothers are caught in conflicting messages between the workplace and home, all of them reinforced by society and its gender binary roles for men and women.

CHAPTER 3

Work is Harder than Ever

Before I returned to work after my first maternity leave, I took my daughter in for an office meet-and-greet. That was the first day my work self and my mother self collided, but it wouldn't be the last. I stood in the elevator with my six-week-old baby, thinking, *I can't take this me in there!*

Everyone was walking and talking fast. Everything around me pulsed with a sense of purpose that I'd been missing and craving, and I was standing in the place that had, up until six weeks before, given me my purpose. And now it all seemed too fast, and kind of frantic.

I can't take this *me* in there!

As I navigated the change in my own life, I couldn't help but notice the pace of change at work was accelerating, and the stakes just kept increasing.

According to Gartner, today's workforce is more distributed and more matrixed, and everyone on the team is suffering from information overload. Laptops, smartphones and videoconferencing have made it possible for more employees to be more *on* more hours, more days of the week. Seventy percent of American workers told *Forbes* they work on the weekend at least once a month.

Or, as Claire Cain Miller put it in *The New York Times,* "women did everything right. Then work got greedy."

American workers log

11%

more hours per year than we did in 1979

Economic Policy Institute, 2013

The United States ranks last.
That's right, dead last.

On average, we're working more than ever. Rather than making it possible to work less, digital connectivity has tethered us more tightly than ever to our work.

Among white collar professionals, salary and job security are increasingly tied to working additional hours, traveling more frequently, and generally being more *available* in roles that used be exempt from hourly scrutiny and extra assignments.

Overall employee engagement is stagnant, holding steady at one-third of employees who feel involved in, enthusiastic about, and committed to their work and workplace.

And among working moms, one eye is always on the horizon, to see if there is a scenario that could be better for her overall work-life situation. It could be as simple as a company that allows working from home or has a shorter commute.

In a global study, UNICEF ranked the U.S. 41st out of 41 developed countries in terms of family-friendly policies, including paid parental leave and child care programs or funding. This makes work even harder for parents, who often return to their jobs too soon, or unpaid, or both.

33%

of U.S. employees are engaged at work, and this number has barely budged for the past 15 years it's been measured by Gallup.

State of the American Workplace, 2016

83%

of working mothers would leave their job for an opportunity that better supports their work and life choices

The Mom Project, 2019

The Motherhood Penalty

A woman's earning power decreases
4% for every child she bears

A man's earning power increases **6%** for every child he adds to his family

The Fatherhood Bonus

Third Way's NEXT Initiative, 2014

Child care costs, on average, $1,000/month.

Per child.

U.S. Department of Agriculture, 2017

Only

17%

of U.S. workers have access
to paid family leave

Bureau of Labor Statistics, 2018

WORKPLACE GRADE CARD

Let's see how your employer stacks up on family-friendly policies and culture.

Culture	☐ Awesome	☐ OK	☐ Ugh
Family Leave	☐ Awesome	☐ OK	☐ Ugh
Return from Leave	☐ Awesome	☐ OK	☐ Ugh
Lactation Support	☐ Awesome	☐ OK	☐ Ugh
Childcare Support	☐ Awesome	☐ OK	☐ Ugh
Flexibility/WFH	☐ Awesome	☐ OK	☐ Ugh
Travel Policy	☐ Awesome	☐ OK	☐ Ugh
Support for Dads	☐ Awesome	☐ OK	☐ Ugh
Support for Adoptive Parents	☐ Awesome	☐ OK	☐ Ugh

WORKING LIKE A MOTHER

When someone asks you, *How's work?* do you light up, or groan? Here are a few questions to help you pinpoint your pain points:

What are you struggling with most at work? _____

_____

_____

Who else on your team is a mom? _____

_____

_____

What resources does your company have for moms? _____

_____

_____

Among your executive leaders, how many are moms? _____

_____

_____

FOR FURTHER READING

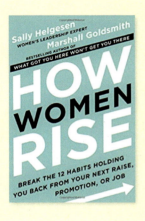

How Women Rise: Break the 12 Habits Holding You Back From Your Next Raise, Promotion, Or Job
By Sally Helgesen and Marshall Goldsmith

This book will help you see how your behavior at work—which was effective until now and you've been conditioned to continue—is actually in your way. In a no-nonsense but non-accusing way, the authors will help set you straight.

Notes: _____
_____
_____
_____
_____

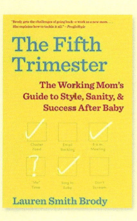

The Fifth Trimester: The Working Mom's Guide to Style, Sanity & Success After Baby
By Lauren Smith Brody

If you're familiar with the parenting books by Dr. Harvey Karp, you'll recognize Brody's analogy—quite simply, that moms are asked to return to work a full trimester before they (or their babies) are ready.

Notes: _____

CHAPTER 4

Homefront, or Front Lines?

It could be that the biggest problem for working moms today is actually what happens at home—or, more accurately, what doesn't happen.

For women, and men, who grew up after the Baby Boom, equality at home was something we all assumed had been fought for and figured out. After all, more women were working. More men were changing diapers.

In my own household, the division of labor seemed totally fine until our first child was born. Completely overwhelmed by the tasks of breastfeeding and infant care, I quickly lost my grip on the laundry and routine cleaning and gardening and maintenance tasks that were usually on my list.

To my great surprise, no one noticed these tasks remaining undone, except me. My newborn certainly didn't care, and my husband said repeatedly he'd be happy to help more if I'd just ask for what I needed.

Instead of being a place I could go to relax, home became a place I had to supervise. Instead of being a relationship I could rely on for comfort or joy, my marriage became a project management position. Instead of being just a little snuggle machine, my baby became another thing I had to take care of on an already long list.

> The biggest problem for working moms is actually what happens at home—or more accurately, what *doesn't* happen.

**HOURS PER DAY
SPENT ON HOUSE TASKS:**

Women: **2.3**

Men: 1.4

Bureau of Labor Statistics, 2019

98

the number of hours worked each week
by the average working mom,
when you include childcare and housework

Working Mother, 2018

65%/35%

child care responsibilities shouldered by working mothers versus working fathers

Pew Research Center and Bureau of Labor Statistics, 2016 and 2018

> I became my own worst enemy, conflicted about my right to ask, self-conscious about my rising anger... I was living like a second-class citizen in my own home.

Darcy Lockman, *All the Rage: Mothers, Fathers and the Myth of Equal Partnership*

The gender gap begins at home.

Even when you try to avoid it, it's there.

When you read about the pay gap and **The Motherhood Penalty** and **The Fatherhood Bonus,** it's easy to get outraged at corporate leadership.

And yet, we are training our daughters to expect the same, given recent data reported in *The New York Times*. Namely:

- Girls do more chores than boys around the house
- Girls make less allowance than boys
- When girls are paid for chores, they are paid less than boys

When we teach girls their leisure time is less valuable than boys', we're reinforcing that they will ultimately do more at home and accept less reward at work.

And it's not just that mothers (and their daughters) are doing more to take care of the home, they're also in charge of all the *seeing what needs done*.

The remembering. The listmaking. The calendar-keeping. The millions of details it takes to keep a family on track, from dentist appointments to permission slips to shopping lists.

Feminists call this *the mental load,* and it's exhausting. A 2017 study showed that 86% of working mothers say they are carrying more than their share of the mental load.

And this is among women who were raised to believe that equal partnerships were possible!

Couples need to be having conversations, *ideally before* their baby is born, about how they are going to divide household tasks to make sure they are equitable.

Claire Kamp Dush, Ph.D.,
Dads Are Often Having Fun While Moms Work Around the House

Women spent 46 to 49 minutes relaxing, while men did child care or housework on their day off.

Men spent about 2x that amount of time in leisure— about 101 minutes— while their partners did some kind of work.

Data via *The New Parents Project,* The Ohio State University

PARTNERSHIP PATTERNS

If you're married or partnered at home, how equal are your roles?

- [ ] Partner does more
- [ ] We're pretty equal
- [ ] Is this a joke?

If your kids are old enough, how much do they help with house tasks?

- [ ] Pretty well for their age
- [ ] Let's just say they're learning
- [ ] My kids? Help?

How do you describe the mental load? *It's OK if there are F-bombs in here.*

[ ]

If you gave up the mental load tomorrow, what would happen at your house?

- [ ] Everyone would be fine, eventually
- [ ] My family would call someone for help
- [ ] Starvation and foreclosure due to library fines

LEISURE TIME

You get a surprise day off from your job—and it's tomorrow.
What would you do with your *free time?*

_____

_____

What are the things you'd still have to do yourself tomorrow (outside of going to work) because it's easier than explaining to your partner or kids?

_____

_____

And if the opposite were true and your partner or kids got the day off tomorrow? How would they spend their time?

_____

_____

FOR FURTHER READING

All the Rage: Mothers, Fathers and the Myth of Equal Partnership
By Darcy Lockman

If you're angry about how the work in your household gets divided up, this book will make you feel better. And if you're not angry yet, this book will piss you off.

You'll find out how common it is in dual earner households for women to do more of the unpaid and care work, and what you can do to ease the burden in your own marriage or parenting situation.

Notes: _____

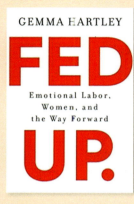

Fed Up: Emotional Labor, Women, and the Way Forward
By Gemma Hartley

This 2018 book came out after Hartley's article by the same name went viral online. She focused on the notion that, "even having a conversation about the imbalance of emotional labor becomes emotional labor," and many readers will relate.

Notes: _____
_____
_____
_____
_____

CHAPTER 5

Parenting Today is Hard AF*

I was not prepared for the overwhelming sense of love I have for both my children. I was not prepared for the sleep deprivation or the challenges of breastfeeding. I was not prepared for the huge sense of responsibility that settled on my shoulders when they handed me those babies and sent us home from the hospital.

But I *really* wasn't prepared for the realization that—in addition to working, doing more than twice the work around our house, and spending as many guilt-ridden moments as possible with my children—I would have to study this much to be a mom.

I didn't realize I would have to study this much to be a mom.

Even with an excellent, down-to-earth pediatrician, an awesome network of mom friends, and the blessing of family within a few miles, I still find that I need a crash course or expert guidance at almost every new age and stage for our daughter and our son.

* *I'm proud of myself for only using one F word in this book, and I managed to abbreviate it in the hippest of current slang* :)

8 in 10

adults say American women face pressure to be *involved parents*

adults say American men face pressure to be *involved parents*

5 in 10

Pew Research Center, 2019

The bar for parents has been raised.
By society, by modern life, and by our kids.

It's not just the role of motherhood that has changed—so has the role of childhood.

As families have evolved and infant mortality rates dropped, each individual child is a protected, precious, desired being, into which parents now pour incredible amounts of resources.

This is not a bad thing.

But it does change the dynamic between busy, employed mothers and children who, increasingly, require time and attention that we perhaps didn't account for when we made the decisions to start our families.

The New York Times recently suggested that women, especially college-educated women, underestimate the personal cost of motherhood.

Meaning, the time it takes to invest in longer periods of breastfeeding, child care coverage in the absence of federal programs for preschool children, and helping children keep up with a dizzying array of enrichment activities and opportunities.

All families are running this race in isolation, without the *village* that used to be there to help.

And that busy calendar? It keeps even close neighbors from knowing or sharing each other's family burdens.

Without the pop-in, without the vibrant presence of neighbors, without life in the cul-de-sacs and the streets, the pressure reverts back to the *nuclear family*

Jennifer Senior, *All Joy And No Fun*

Nearly half of grandparents live 5+ hours

away...

...from their grandchildren.

AARP, 2019

42%

of children 8 and younger
have their own tablet device

Common Sense Media, 2017

20%

of school-aged children are in some way neurologically diverse, meaning how their brains function is *atypical* from what's considered *normal*.

Deborah Reber, Founder of *TiLT Parenting* and author of *Differently Wired*

The stress of parenting in a modern age is intensified if you have a child with any sort of special need—and that could include a whole host of concerns beyond just medical issues:

- Giftedness
- Autism
- Asperger's Syndrome
- Sensory Processing Disorder
- ADD/ADHD
- Dyslexia
- Anxiety/Depression
- *Twice Exceptional* *kids with two or more of the above*

Let's talk about youth sports.

This $15 billion dollar industry in the U.S. has taken a major front seat in the lives of modern families—practices, games, travel teams, snack schedules, team photos—and that's just the junior levels! Who knew an endeavor that was supposed to teach our kids team values would end up costing us family time?

> We have elevated sports into a *cultural religion*

Dr. James Emery White, *Parents, Sports and Church*

RAISING KIDS IS A TEAM SPORT

1. Village Roll Call!
In a pinch, who could you call to help?

AT HOME

_____
_____
_____

AT WORK

_____
_____
_____

2. Who is doing the same tasks you're doing?
Can you combine forces to help each other?

AT HOME

_____
_____
_____

AT WORK

_____
_____
_____

BY DESIGN, NOT DEFAULT

Have you taken the time to chart a course for your family's priorities? This can dramatically help when it comes to making decisions on children's technology use, sports participation, and the overall use of your family's time and attention.

WHAT ARE YOUR FAMILY'S TOP VALUES?

In our family, we believe in _____

_____

_____

_____

What do you want to add?	What could you let go of?

FOR FURTHER READING

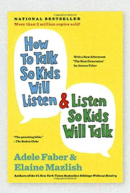

How to Talk So Kids Will Listen & Listen So Kids Will Talk
By Adele Faber & Elaine Mazlish

This book provides a clear understanding of how to understand your child's feelings, and share your own, in a respectful way that is all new for our generation of parents. I listened to this via Audible and cried multiple times in the first chapter *alone*.

Differently Wired: Raising an Exceptional Child in a Conventional World
By Deborah Reber

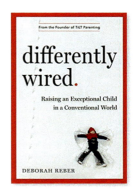

Even without full data and reporting, we know that 20% of kids classify as not being "neurotypical," meaning their brains are wired to learn and respond differently than the mainstream. This makes parenting a challenge, to say the least. If you need it, this book will help.

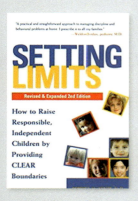

Setting Limits
By Dr. Robert McKenzie

At the heart of the positive parenting movement lies this book (and its sister title: *Setting Limits with Your Strong-Willed Child*, the one we needed at our house). This was recommended to us by the Director of Early Childhood Programs at our children's preschool, and it's a lifesaver.

Unselfie: Why Empathetic Kids Succeed in our All-About-Me World
By Michele Borba, Ed.D.

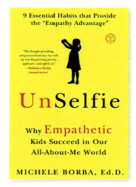

This book came our way after a growth mindset seminar at our daughter's school. The principal was reading it with her senior staff, and highly recommended it. In full disclosure, it's still on my list but I haven't read it yet.

CHAPTER 6

The Way Forward for Today's Moms

At a recent event, I ran into a friend who is a successful executive with two beautiful daughters. I asked her how she was doing.

She sighed and said, "I'm fine. I mean, I'm half-assing everything, but I'm fine."

After we talked, I couldn't stop thinking about what she said. I felt it too, the nagging sense that I wasn't doing a good job as a mother or an executive.

Like I was failing my kids and my colleagues. I had heard women express this before. We talked about it at book club, in Facebook Groups, in the hallways. We shared it with our friends and maybe our spouses, but not with our bosses. We didn't dare let this feeling be uttered at work for fear that people would see us as less-than-engaged.

Most of the time, we said it like a joke. But the more research I did, the less I felt like laughing.

I'm half-assing everything, but I'm fine.

> I think while all mothers deal with feelings of guilt, working mothers are plagued by *guilt on steroids!*

Arianna Huffington, Founder & CEO, *Thrive Global*

87%

of mothers feel guilty for some aspect
of their parenting or working lives

Nuk, via *The Guardian,* 2017

The kids will be alright.
But we're right to be worried about the moms.

I wondered if the *motherhood* social media conversation reflected this overwhelming majority. I looked in my own Facebook Moms Groups, and I asked a former colleague with access to some social media listening tools to help me as well.

To my surprise, only 12% of the conversation actually used the word *guilt*.

The scariest part to me was this discrepancy. How working moms were afraid to say it out loud. How silenced we had become by the mixed messages in social media and from male-dominated workforces, how alone we were with this feeling that was actually almost universal.

Social science researcher Caitlyn Collins studied mothers in four countries, and found that mothers in the U.S. were the least happy in their dual roles, and the most stressed. Collins even went so far as to characterize U.S. working moms as being in a state of crisis.

The work-family conflict experienced by mothers makes it hard to feel successful at either role. And it brings no joy or justice to our families, our companies, or ourselves for a majority of women to walk around feeling guilty.

In fact, together with the isolation and lack of support, it contributes to postpartum depression and postpartum anxiety.

> American moms stood apart for not only their stress and their worry, but they were the only women that I interviewed who didn't expect to have external supports from their employers, from their partners or from the federal government.

Caitlyn Collins, *Making Motherhood Work*

1 in 7

mothers experience
Postpartum Depression

American Psychological Association, 2007

Postpartum Anxiety is

3x

more prevalent than Postpartum Depression, but less understood and often undiagnosed

University of British Columbia, 2016

How has social media raised the bar on work and parenting?

Which social channels make you feel like you're less than perfect as a mom/partner/employee?

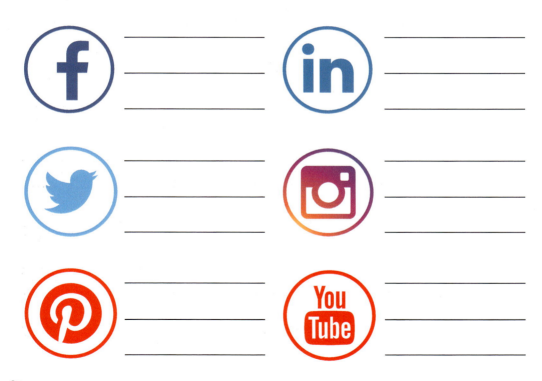

How often do you relate to these statements, on a spectrum from *always* to *never*? These questions will help you learn more about how high your expectations really are—for yourself and others.

I feel guilty about my choices based on what I see from other moms or colleagues.	ALWAYS	NEVER
I feel more pressure to be perfect at home that at work.	ALWAYS	NEVER
I present my real life in social media—good and bad.	ALWAYS	NEVER
I judge myself more harshly than others when it comes to parenting or work issues.	ALWAYS	NEVER
When I check social media, I am left feeling better/happier/lighter.	ALWAYS	NEVER
My own definition of a *good mom* or *good employee* is swayed by social media.	ALWAYS	NEVER
I feel like more is expected of me—at home and at work—than of moms before me.	ALWAYS	NEVER

GET MORE RECOGNITION

A little recognition can go a long way. You're constantly building skills in your kids by affirming what they do accomplish, right? What about for yourself? What would really make you feel seen in this chaotic phase of work-life conflict? Do you want flowers? Verbal compliments or affirmations? Kids who say *thank you?* A gold star sticker chart?

As grown women and the nerve centers of our households, we probably have to guide our families on what we need. Try not to roll your eyes but really think about how you'd like to be appreciated—and by whom—for all you're doing.

Whose recognition would mean the most?	What would that recognition look like?

SO NOW WHAT?

Every age and stage of your children, every scenario of your career will look and operate a little differently. You can't fix it all in one day and your needs will change as your situation evolves.

Use these questions to point you toward what would help the most right now, including some tough conversations with a boss, a partner, or even your kids.

 It's harder at home   It's harder at work   They're equally hard

What do you most need (only choose 1-2, so you can focus your efforts):

- I need validation and support, and a place to tell my story
- I need a better emotional relief valve than what I've been using so far
- I need a deeper understanding of my family's history & expectations for working motherhood
- I need my family to get with the times and adjust their expectations to match modern life
- I need to find my *tribe* at work—the other moms on my team, in my department, or in company leadership
- I need to reconsider where I'm working, based on their willingness to support working moms

- I need more help at home, from the mental load to the daily tasks
- I need a way to share or relieve my anger at the imbalance at home
- I need more knowledge or resources for parenting
- I need a stronger, more activated village around me
- I need to talk to a doctor or therapist about PPD or PPA
- I need to take a break from social media
- I need to ask for more recognition

FOR FURTHER READING/LISTENING

Moms Don't Have Time To Read Books
Hosted by Zibby Owens

A quick summary of the latest books, via author interviews and commentary. This will help you feel caught up and in-the-know.

All Joy and No Fun: The Paradox of Modern Parenthood
By Jennifer Senior

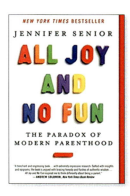

This was the first book to capture what so many modern moms were afraid to say out loud: Is this how it's supposed to feel?! In her groundbreaking work, Senior turns the age-old question around to ask what children do to their parents' lives and marriages. This one is a must-read (or must-skim, if you're like me!)

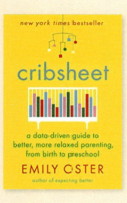

Cribsheet: A Data-Driven Guide to Better, More Relaxed Parenting, from Birth to Preschool
By Emily Oster, Ph.D.

A Brown University economist takes on the truth, via reams and reams of data, about everything from breastfeeding to vaccinations.

Notes: _____

Acknowledgements

Thank you to all my workshop participants, focus group participants, peer groups and professional groups, moms' groups, and friends who have given me their perspective on their current work-life collision.

To Jenn, thank you for being a strategic partner at the start, and ultimately bringing this book across the finish line and making it so beautiful.

Thank you to the authors and podcasters whose work I've listed here—your research and storytelling have made this issue more clear for moms today, and everyone around us.

To Alaina, for pushing me to give the first *tell-all* talk and tell my story.

I'm grateful to **Mindstream Interactive and Julie Sablar** for the social listening that helped me understand the mom conversation in social media.

To **Ami and Brian at Hopewell,** for always holding space for me.

Beth and Yasmine, you have inspired me and pushed me and helped me make a**'parent**ly into a reality. Thank you.

Thank you to my **mom and dad,** for your unwavering support this summer and always.